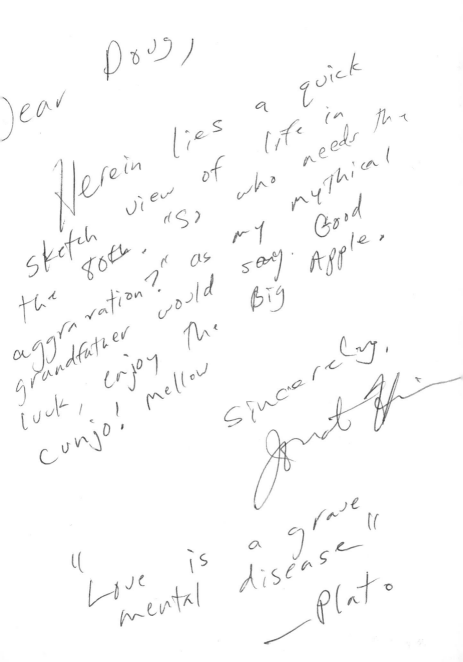

Dear Doug,

Herein lies a quick sketch view of life in the 80th. "So who needs the aggravation?" as my mythical grandfather would say. Good luck, enjoy the Big Apple. Mellow cunjo!

Sincerely,

Janet Sh...

"Love is a grave mental disease"
— Plato

Nukes Are People, Too

NUKES
ARE PEOPLE, TOO

A Comedy Book?

Jonathan Lindley Harris

VANTAGE PRESS
New York / Washington / Atlanta
Los Angeles / Chicago

Illustrated by Ken Landgraf

FIRST EDITION

Copyright © 1987 by Jonathan Lindley Harris

Published by Vantage Press, Inc.
516 West 34th Street, New York, New York 10001

Manufactured in the United States of America
ISBN: 0-533-07054-6

Nukes Are People, Too

On the Handicapped

Nothing against the handicapped, but why is it that they get all of the best parking spaces? Is that fair? It must be that Reagan; he is just too damn soft on everyone.

On Intellectuals

Wouldn't you like to see great intellectuals making fools of themselves? Gore Vidal in a cowboy suit. William F. Buckley cheering wildly at a Yankees game, wearing a baseball cap. George Will driving a Malibu race car, wearing a childish grin.

On Rock Stars

What kind of homes do rock stars live in? Colonial? English Tudor? I just can't see David Lee Roth entering a big white colonial dressed in his usual attire, but God knows he can afford them. Do they trash their houses, like they do hotel rooms?

Is Sting really a genius? No doubt there. The next Shelley, a real visionary.

On the Ancient Greeks

Historians have been debating the question for centuries: "Just what did kill off the ancient Greeks? Was it the Visigoths? Was it the Romans?" I think we now have the proper information to surmise the answer: AIDS.

On Outer Space

Space exploration, what a big hype! Why are we spending millions of dollars just to float around up there? We found out the moon was just a big dumb rock. And everyone knows the sun is just a big space heater that doesn't even work half of the year.

On Suicide

Can a failed suicide be tried for attempted murder?

Why is it that women usually commit suicide with sleeping pills? What a bunch of sissies. If they were really liberated, they would shoot themselves the way men do. That's something that women's lib should be working on.

On Europe

England is like a whole country of stand up comedians. Even the stewards on British airlines deliver a twenty-minute monologue over the intercom.

The highways in Europe all resemble the Indy 500. I kept thinking I had accidently stumbled onto the highway for race drivers in training and kept looking for the regular roads.

The people all look like they are in a rock video. They don't walk the streets; they pose.

And they use all that funny money over there, oversized and brightly colored, and the people all play along as if it's real money. I guess they're all in on the joke.

They live in all those old buildings made of brick; haven't they even heard about modern architecture?

A lot of them complain about poverty, overcrowding, or pollution. What's the gripe? A lot of people have never even been to Europe.

On Americans

A lot of Americans seem to think that we are the only free country in the world. Outside of our boundaries there are: 1) Russia (boo-hiss), and 2) those small countries full of torture all run by homicidal dictators (like Iran and various American nations). It's all like "out there." (And we think Russia has a lot of propaganda.)

What is Europe? A totalitarian nation? Or because it's just a Disneyland for the rich, it doesn't really count?

On Air Travel

We send people to psychiatrists if they are afraid of flying. Is this sound? Because a person is afraid to go up in the air thousands of feet, hundreds of miles an hour, in infallible metal boxes that invariably crash, flown by drunk-sounding macho Texans, they are neurotic?

It's the metal that bothers me. If planes were covered in feathers it would be a lot more soothing psychologically.

What do birds think when they see airplanes? Do they nudge each other and have a good belly laugh?

On the Penal System

It is apparent that the penal system in America is not working very well. For most inmates, incarceration only solidifies their bitterness with society.

Here's an idea: Hardened criminals should be forced to read the classics of western literature. Pimps could be coerced to stay home on Friday and Saturday nights to read Milton or Spenser. Who knows? They may learn to like it!

"Man, I've been reading this cat Dante. Real heavy dude."

"Dante? Man, he ain't cool. I've been reading Milton, the blind genius, man. He's like Stevie Wonder."

On Street People

In Los Angeles, the street people sometimes walk twenty or thirty miles a day. You can see one in Santa Monica and in Hollywood later in the same day. Where do they go? Why don't they just stay put? Are they in training for the walking event in the Olympics?

These poor people. I once had a woman grab a piece of pizza right out of my hands at an outdoor "Piece of Pizza." What could be going through their minds when they see advertisements for Rolls Royces or homes in Bel Air: Maybe next year? Talk about salt in the wound.

On the NBA

The National Basketball Association has begun to resemble the Harlem Globetrotters. The white guys are the straight men, making blasé passes and standing around looking bored or dumbfounded while the black stars carry out the show. Save for Larry Bird, who looks like a white guy failing miserably at a funky dance step; despite it all, he puts every ball in the hoop.

On Work

The real problem with work is that they pay you with a boring check, instead of cold, hard cash. A check has no emotional content. At the end of every week, they should pay employees with greenbacks, counting out each bill as it hits your palm, while all the other employees scream out in tandem with the boss, "200, 400, 600!," just like on a game show. Now that would surely increase worker productivity.

On Gays

I read that there was a gay riot in San Francisco. Isn't that a contradiction in terms?

"Hit me, don't touch me."
"Beat me, don't touch me, you animal."

I would like to see gays working in a very macho environment, such as an all gay staff at the Pep Boys. "At the Pep Boys, Manny, Moe, and Jacques."

"Pass me the oil can, honey."
"Get it yourself, bitch."

On Jews

There just aren't enough Jewish alcoholics or Jewish wife beaters. No wonder they are so neurotic. They don't let it out.

How do we know that Jesus was really Jewish? His mother worshipped him and he went into his father's business.

On the Eighties

Everything is out in the open now; how boring. No longer are social conflicts swept under the rug. Nobody moves to Greenwich Village anymore and changes their name from Robert Zimmerman to Bob Dylan and becomes a Jewish cowboy. We've really taken the romance out of being a minority.

The eighties are very hard line. The other day I saw someone driving slowly in front of an amblance. Soon bumper stickers will read, "Save the Nukes," "Corrupt and Loving It," "Kill Authority," and "Nukes Are People, Too."

On Doctors

Even our caring physicians have grown callous and greedy. Do you feel insulted when you go to a doctor's office and all of the Reserved for Doctor spaces are filled with Mercedes and you're driving a Toyota?

If you refuse to leave a doctor's office until you are well healed, the nurse will tell you, "Only the doctors leave here in that condition."

I once caused so much trouble on the operating table that the doctor stomped out of the room and replied, "Suit yourself."

And why is it that all doctors have bad breath? Is there an exam they must pass certifying that their breath be dreadful enough before they go into practice?

On Christmas

Just whose holiday is Christmas, anyway? Santa's or Jesus'? It's gotten so commercial you can't tell anymore. I imagine they argue about it:

"Get out of my holiday."
"Your holiday? What do you know about snow and presents, you desert rat?"
"What do you know about saving the world?"
"Man, do you have delusions of grandeur."
"Listen fatty, I've had about enough of you. Take off that silly outfit, drop 100 pounds, and get a real job."

On Black People

Were Adam and Eve white or black? I need to ask a black minister that one.

Are blacks interested in space exploration? I haven't seen a lot of interest on their part. But imagine the possibilities—slam-dunking at 300 feet.

But would their mothers allow them to go up in space? "Uh-uh, baby. Don't you go up in no spaceship, baby. You know that stuff is all fake. If God had wanted you to fly. . . "

Does Gary Coleman resent Mr. T for having stolen his act and spruced it up with violence? Does Chesterfield resent them both for stealing his act?

A few years back, there was an irate black man who took some hostages in a gas station and made these two demands: 1) That all white people leave the face of the earth in twenty-four hours' time, and 2) that all money be burned. Obviously, he was not to happy with his lot in life. And eventually he was apprehended and sent to a mental institution, where they assured him that there was nothing wrong with being poor and oppressed.

But the police had grave trouble apprehending him. All of that could have been avoided if Walter Cronkite would have come on the evening news and announced, "All white people are now leaving the planet earth," accompanied by Hollywood footage of white people piling into space ships with saddened expressions, waving good-bye. And with footage of large circles of rich people in the suburbs, smiling and burning piles of money. It could have been set to music like a rock video and directed by Spielberg. Then the whole public could have been let in on the joke.

But which is more likely—money-burning or leaving the planet?

On Television

Television has done a lot of mixing social and cultural groups; in fact, it has brought them all together for the

11

first time in history. Now that is a dangerous idea, and you can expect some hypocrisy.

When blacks watch movies like *Trading Places*, do they think, *Boy, I just love those rich, exploitive white people; they're so cute?* Does the happy ending placate them?

Or when rich people watch the "Dukes of Hazzard," do they think *I just love those good old boys; I'd love to spend time carousing with them.* Or, more likely, do they think, *I'd really like to have them working for me at the factory; they're such good strong lifters.*
And why is it that the Dukes always climb out of the windows of their car? What is wrong with the doors?

Why is the judge on television programs always a black, handicapped woman? Sure, there are a lot of liberals in Hollywood, but isn't this overkill?

And why are the police chiefs always fat black men who like to kick young white rookie smart alecks around but who secretly "love those guys," despite the fact that they break all the rules?

Why is the band on "Name that Tune" so awful? I couldn't identify the national anthem with them playing it ten minutes. How is anyone supposed to guess those tunes?

On Looks

I have to think that people's appearances must have a lot to do with their performance in life. If Albert Einstein had looked like Tom Selleck, would he have developed the theory of relativity? If Woody Allen looked like Robert

Redford, would he be funny? And if David Letterman did not look like Alfred E. Neuman, would he be such a sarcastic buffoon?

On Reagan

Reagan has twelve basic tenets to his philosophy:

1) Welfare has ruined America, and the recipients are all fakers and whiners.
2) All rich people are oppressed.
3) A limited nuclear war in Europe might be fun. (Despite the loss of historic monuments, which could be deterred with the neutron route.) But the survivability and winnability looked exciting until one of his advisers told him about this thing called *fallout*. (They didn't have any stupid fallout in the good old cowboy shoot-outs).
4) Racism in America was a little thing in the fifties, which has since been cured, and Martin Luther King was a militant, treasonous, card-carrying communist. Just what was his big gripe anyways? (Ronnie hasn't seen *Roots* yet.)

5) There is no racism in South Africa. They cured their problem, too. Those silly riots are unfair to the whites who have done so much for reform.

6) The marines are a beautiful, sentimental outfit (*Semper F.*); Rambo is a saint; *Red Dawn* was a realistic epic, full of valor and heroism. It brings tears to the eyes.

7) The schools are wild dens of iniquity, full of drugs and sex. (He saw *The Blackboard Jungle*.) Nancy is "very concerned about this, too."

8) "Nuclear war cannot and should not ever be fought" became his second-term public relations chant, despite the fact that the bombing begins in five minutes revealed his wonderful sense of humor, and who knew anyone was listening? How unfair to eavesdrop on a president joking with the boys.

9) Nuclear weapons can be repelled by staying in your basement and/or using an umbrella. Besides, if you can't handle a little explosion, where are your *cajones*?

10) Christian prayer in the schools can solve any problem we might have. Especially since the enemy is godless.

11) Minorities are cute, especially Mr. T. and Gary Coleman. Nancy likes them, too.

12) Gun control is unfair to people who like to be shot (like himself).

Why must we have a president who has a ranch? Does the president of France have a ranch?

And why must we have an actor in the White House? Next term, I'm voting for Pee Wee Herman. Chances are he's more mature.

On Violence in the World

How about all of these serial murderers? Remember how shocked we were by Charlie Manson? Today, Manson

would not even get front page news. We've got serial murders by the hundreds: Cult killers, voodoo killers, sex killers, extra-terrestrial killers. Some of them make Manson look like a baby with a tack hammer.

And how about the assassination wave? Poor Sadat got shot right on television. And, what's worse, on a folding chair. Now that's a poor country that puts the heads of state on folding chairs. Someone ought to sue that chair company; they didn't prove to be too sturdy.

It must be embarrassing to be shot right on television. First it was JFK, then Bobby Kennedy, then Reagan. But Reagan didn't seem to mind much. He kept right on smiling, the consummate thespian. And afterwards, he never mentioned it again. Too macho to take note of a silly bullet. "Nothin' but a little flesh wound, ma'am. Saddle me up a pony, won't 'cha, little lady?" Of course, Brady wasn't quite as lucky, but, "Hell, he'll be OK."

Who even remembers that Reagan was shot? There's been so many of them, who can keep track? And the whole thing was so Hollywood, it was about as real as a cartoon.

Ford was shot at on television, but he received much lower ratings. But true, to be stalked by the Manson family is a thing of status. I wonder if Ford and Reagan ever compared notes:

"I got a seven point share, Ronnie."

"That's nothing, I got a twelve point share. Better luck next time."

"I never came off well on the tube."

"Well, Gerry, that's show biz."

The pope got shot and forgave his assassin. How unchristian can you get?

Soon it will be like the last days of the Roman Empire. We'll be receiving the news of someone's election along with the news of their execution.

On the Psycho Assassin

They invariably catch the psycho who did the shooting, and it's always the same story. "Space dog vampire wolves from Mt. St. Helenes in outer space forced me to shoot him." Why don't they just give these people a job writing for the *National Enquirer*? Forget prison and the long road to rehabilitation; utilize their talents.

On Nukes

In the sixties, we were running around with signs that read, "Ban the Bomb." Boy, were we dumb. We thought there was only one. Didn't we realize that they had built some 40,000 of them since WW II? (Known affectionately as the Big One, it sounds like a sandwich from Burger King.)

The crossbow was outlawed in the Middle Ages. It was considered too dangerous, and many feared it would bring about the end of the world. We've come a long way, baby. Now we have them in museums because they are so cute and harmless.

And why is chemical warfare considered so unethical? What are nukes—fair play? Why slight chemicals? Not macho enough? Not enough blood? Too sneaky? Are there rules in an Armageddon?

Why are there all these anti-nuke protestors around today? What are they—pro-napalm? Pro-tanks? Why be so specific about nukes? Why aren't they anti-war? Nukes don't kill people; people kill people.

Or is it just that "anti-war" has a bad ring to it, still conjuring up images of that God-awful peace movement in the sixties. Those insane peaceniks who wanted peace on earth; what a bunch of sickies. There is advertising and public relations to think of when dealing with the homicidal.

17

Didn't those peaceniks realize that when you try and break up a fight, there's a good chance you'll catch a few fists in the process? Perhaps this dawned on them after Kent State or Chicago. "If you can't beat 'em, join 'em" is the yuppie credo. I guess they weren't as dumb as they looked.

Well, thank God that awful peace movement is over with. Now we can get back to the business of war. That's the beauty of peacetime. It's a nice time-out that gives all sides a good opportunity to gear up for the next one, perfecting and upgrading the weaponry.

On WW II

The Russians are still very upset about World War II (The Big One). They're always threatening us that we won't get off as easy next time.

But the Japanese are so inscrutable. America drops two bombs on them and they never mention it again. "Okay, you win. So sorry." And never another word from them. They're probably putting little H-bombs in our radios. With a two-year timer.

America refused to give the secret to the atomic bomb to Russia after World War II. It's a little like being in a snowball fight and your partner pulls out a blow torch and melts down the enemy. "Gee, that's neat. Can I see it?" "No, get your own." Well they did, all right. It's funny how allies become enemies so quickly when one side gets a new weapon.

Of course the whole problem is that evil empire over there—just ask the president. If only we could wipe them out, we could relax and live in utopia. There'd never be another tyranny, or a threat to society, and life here would run as smooth as a baby's bottom.

On Star Wars

What's all this talk of star wars? What is this, a kid's movie? How can sixty-year-old men sit around in suits in an expensive office and seriously discuss Star Wars? And how do the newsmen keep a straight face when they deliver the idea to the public? Don't they even giggle a little at the notion? And George Lucas doesn't even get any residuals?

On Nuclear Winter

My biggest fear of nuclear winter is this: What to wear? Is a ski parka appropriate? Or something more formal, like a Chesterfield? I wouldn't want to underdress for an Armageddon. And how are the ski conditions?

On Neutron Bombs

I'm all for them. At least leave Notre Dame or Westminister Abbey. Maybe even the Kremlin or the Great Wall.

On Laughing Gas

Not a bad idea. Let's put some humor into WW III, the super big one. Why not send Bob Hope over there with it for added comic relief.

On Mutually Assured Destruction

A stroke of genius. Two guns pointed at each other's heads. Makes life fun and worry free. Kind of like a policeman on a big scale; unfortunately the scale is way out of bounds. Do we need MAD 100 times over? Yet despite the overkill, they're still talking buildup. It's like shooting mosquitoes with a canon. But it is reassuring to know that as you fry, the bad guys do too. Good for the ego.

On Reduction

You drop your gun, then I'll drop mine. Sure thing. Remember, this has nothing to do with peace, only outsmarting. The war is still on.

On The Day After

Why do we need a low budget TV movie with a plot as slow as molasses to convince us that nuclear exchange may not be a lot of laughs? Yet here are some actual responses to the film:

"It was boring. I can take my ten-year-old to see more killings in *Star Wars.*" (Not enough action for him; how disassociated can you get?)

"It's all just government propaganda to make you think the world is ending so you'll go out and spend a lot of money."(K-Mart, open up those gates to paradise.)

Both these items were seen in the *Kentucky Enquirer*. (Kentucky is not a hotbed for intellectualism.)

A friend remarked, "Judging from that movie, it would be horrible. Like a living hell." What did he think before the movie, that it would be a swim party with a bad thunderstorm? Talk about lacking an imagination.

On the Present State of War

It's all gotten so confusing. What are the new mechanics of this war thing? For example, if they went with chemicals, would we have to go with nukes? If they went with conventional, would we go with chemicals? Or with nukes? Or both? Or if they went with star wars, would we go with chemicals, nukes, stars wars, or a combination of the three? If they went with chemicals, how would we know? It could already be in our drinking water and into our precious bodily fluids. Could we immediately counter with nukes, or would it be too late? What if they went with brainwashing, or already have? Everyone knows that rock music is a communist plot. Oh, why worry needlessly over a silly thing like choices? I'm sure they'll get it figured out.

This whole war thing has gotten so confusing; all of the rules of the game have been changed so fast. I long for the simpler days, all swords and boiling oil, or the bow and arrow and the blowgun. Those were the days. Men were men, toe to toe, and women were proud of it.

Now it's a little like ordering a Coke. Do I want old Coke Classic, new, cherry, diet, salt-free . . . ?

And to think that future wars can be fought sitting in the comfort of your own living room. Just push a few buttons. Now that's what I call convenience. It's even better than remote-control television and drive-through restaurants. "Use it once; it works while you sleep." Kills bugs dead.

On the Reality of WW III

Will the superpowers ever be the ones to drop those nukes or activate the star wars? Who knows? But history has shown that guns rarely stay on shelves, that curiousity killed the cat, and that paranoia, boredom, and frustration can lead to a pretty bad end.

But who cares anymore? Most people seem to be in a daze, trying to stay happy and amused, hoping all these bad vibes don't hit the fan. But for right now, we're content to just sit back and watch the little guys fight it out on television. (With a little help from their friends, of course.) Great action footage on the news, almost as good as Hollywood, but not quite as realistic.

Will the superpowers continue to shadow-box in strange little territories? Which, if either, is really trying to take over the world? Will the little hotheads obliterate one another? Will that bring the superpowers closer together, or push them farther apart? And would the superpowers join together in the event of an attack from outer space? Stay tuned for the next episode of *How the World Explodes*.

On the Distant Future

Assuming that all the hardware stays up on the shelf where it belongs, nukes and the whole ball of wax will no doubt become obsolete. We'll probably have lasers that can wipe out the entire galaxy by voice command. For a while, nukes may be marketed for home use, until they disappear altogether. Then they will take their place in a museum along side the cross bow, the tank, and the fighter plane. Families will view them for amusement:

"Look, honey, those things were called nukes. They could only destroy one planet at a time and people thought

23

they were dangerous. What a laugh."

"Mommy, they're funny-looking. Were they ever used?"

"Just a few times, dear. Nothing serious."

The Christian religion seems to be out of the war thing now; I think the governments kicked them out. It's just as well; they grew tired of the whole thing once those fun swords were gone. It really took the sport out of it. Now all those weird Eastern religions and sects run the show.

It looks like the only way out is space. We're getting too crowded here to ever get along. For the sake of aliens, we ought to post a sign at the Equator: "Planet Earth. Enter at your own risk. Familiarity breeds contempt."

Someday we'll probably be living on some other planet or in space stations (if we survive). Then we can put a glass bubble over the whole earth and use it as a museum piece. (Everything becomes a museum piece eventually.) Visitors from Mars can view it the way we view ancient ruins or log cabins.

"Look honey, it was the first home for humans; it kind of makes you nostalgic. Look at those things they called trees. And look, they had machines that traveled on the ground. Now that is a hoot."

But seriously folks, I kid this planet a lot, but I love it.